TURNING YOUR
CHILD'S FAILURES
INTO
SUCCESS

By

Jim Wideman
Jimwideman.com

Turning Your Child's Failures Into Success
By Jim Wideman
Copyright ©2009 by Jim Wideman
Jim Wideman Ministries, Inc.
2441 Q Old Fort Parkway #354
Murfreesboro, TN 37128

ISBN: 978-0-88144-506-0
Published 2009
jim**wideman**.com

TABLE OF CONTENTS

THANKS

There are not enough words to communicate my thanks to my wonderful family. There's no way to write parenting books without a family to practice on. I guess some have tried it but it's a lot more fun growing, loving and doing life together. Thanks for letting me share your stories with others! You are my greatest sermon! I could not be the parent I desire to be without my wonderful wife and partner, Julie in my life. Thanks again for making me better at everything and for your love and support over all these years. Thanks for believing in me always and encouraging me to write this book. Special thanks are also in order to my fabulous kids; Yancy, Cory and Whitney. Thanks Yancy for being the first child, and let us practice on you. Thanks Cory for loving Yancy and joining our family. Thank you Whitney for being the baby and for just being you. It was fun to parent you girls when you were little but it is an honor to get to continue to parent you now. It's exciting to see the wonderful Godly adults you have become! I am so proud of you! I also want to thank my wonderful church family World Outreach Church in Murfreesboro, TN and Pastor Allen Jackson for opening your hearts and making a place for me. It's an honor to walk out our dreams together.

INTRODUCTION

After more than thirty years of children's ministry, I have not only ministered to children, but I have also spent just as much time training adult leaders. I know that there are only a few called to full-time children's ministry in the church, but everyone who has a child is called to a different form of children's ministry—parenting. Since I have raised two daughters of my own, I understand the need for quality parenting resources; so my goal is to provide you with a guidebook that specifically targets issues parents face on a regular basis.

When my first daughter was born, I resolved in my heart that I would do whatever it took to develop a quality relationship with her. If that meant I had to learn how to enjoy shopping or handing over the television remote, then that was okay (yes, it *is* possible for a man to do these things). With time, I even started watching home-decorating programs and cooking channels, and I enjoyed them too! Girl-world turned out to not be so bad after all.

In my first book for parents, *Connect With Your Kids,* I give simple steps parents can follow to build lasting relationships with their children. *Turning Your Child's Failures Into Success* is the next installment of life lessons any parent can immediately apply. In this book, I tackle one of the most important aspects to failure that all parents should know: Your failures do not keep you from success; how you choose to deal with those failures determines if you're successful or not.

When you realize that the mistakes you make do not keep you from accomplishing your God-given purpose, then how you handle each mistake will be greatly altered. You see, what you do after the mistake determines whether you'll go forward or backward. When we understand that failure is not what keeps a person from succeeding, then failure simply becomes a launching pad for success.

Once we as parents learn how to fail forward, we can properly train our children to do the same. Your kids may be toddlers, elementary age, or even in high school, but it's never too late to begin modeling the right way to fail in front of your children.

CHAPTER 1

NO ONE IS PERFECT

I am originally from Alabama, and like Forest Gump, my mama told me important things all the time. One thing she told me a lot was, "Jim, don't make the same mistake twice. There are enough different ones you can make every time." Over the years I have found that to be true. In fact, I have made so many mistakes that things are actually starting to go right in my life. I'm not alone. Everyone makes mistakes they can learn from.

Have you ever made a mistake as a parent? I mean, really blew it big time? You're not alone either. We have all made mistakes and blown it as parents. Good parents are out there, but "perfect parents" don't exist. Good parents realize that when they make mistakes, it's an opportunity to learn and improve and not a time to wallow in their failures.

If there is no such thing as a perfect parent, then there is no such thing as a perfect child either.

Yes, that's right. Your children are not perfect.

I am sure many of you are nodding your head right now agreeing with me, but I know better. When I was a school administrator, I had to call parents into my office to discuss a situation their child was involved in, and many times their reactions were as follows:

"My child did what?"

"No, not my little Susie."

"What? No, not my perfect child."

Parents, listen to me. My kids aren't perfect and neither are yours.

Let's face it. Our children are just like us. In fact, I have even spent time working to make sure my two girls don't turn out like me. But over time, I have come to realize the things they do that drive me the craziest are the things that they learned from me.

Parents are not perfect. Kids are not perfect. We all make mistakes. That means what we do when we fail is what really counts.

One of my favorite commercials in the whole world is about Michael Jordan. In the commercial it lists the failures in Jordan's life. Did you know he missed more than 9,000 shots? That's a lot of shots. He lost almost 300 games. Now, that's something we don't hear about very much. Twenty-six times he had the chance at the last buzzer to take the game-winning shot, and he missed. In his life, he has failed time and again, but that's why he succeeds. It's not the fact that he made mistakes; it's the fact that he used the mistakes to propel him forward.

Just like Jordan, we will fail. We will make mistakes. In fact, Psalms 34:19 says, "Many are the afflictions of the righteous." A lot of people stop right here and say,

"Oh boy, do I have troubles! I've really blown it!"

But look at the rest of the verse, "But the Lord delivereth him out of them all."

You must choose to be a victor and not a victim. Like Michael Jordon, use your mistakes to propel you forward. Not only will that bring greater success in your life, it will serve as a guide for your children. How you handle mistakes becomes a model for your children to learn how to handle their own mistakes.

When you use your mistakes to propel you forward, your children learn to do the same. When they make a mistake, they will follow your example and evaluate their choices as well. Soon, each mistake they make will be followed with the thought, *Okay, I made a mistake, but what I do next is more important.* When both parents and children understand and apply this principle, it equips the whole family to fulfill their God-given destiny.

CHAPTER 2

LIVING MODELS

How many of you remember hearing this: "Do as I say, not as I do"? As parents, we have a responsibility to do more than just give our children lip service. We cannot continue saying, "You do this while I do that." This kind of thinking riled up my generation: we shot the peace sign and grew our hair out three feet. But kids today are not like the longhaired hippies; they are shorthaired hippies. They don't shoot the peace sign; they shoot one another. Surprisingly, the thing that has them riled up is the same thing that had my generation riled up. They are tired of people saying, "Here's one set of rules for you, and here's another set for me."

It's your job as a parent to be a living model for your children in all things. This includes training them how to handle mistakes. A lot of parents focus on teaching their children how to do right, but they don't teach them what to do if they fail. When children make a bad decision, rather than listening to the Word, many will follow their peer's example of how to fix it. As parents, we must be the ones doing the training, not our children's friends.

The process to training our children how to fail forward begins when we as parents step onto the runway of life and model our decisions.

Some of you may be saying, "But I bring my kids to church. Isn't that what the children's pastor is supposed to do?" Well, let's look at what

God's Word says about that. In Deuteronomy 6:6 niv it says, "These commandments that I give you today are to be upon your hearts." Who is God talking to in this verse? He's talking to His people, the children of Israel. If He's talking to His people, then He's talking to us too. We the parents are to follow God's commandments, not just our children.

Look at the first part of verse seven, "Impress them on your children." Whose job is that? Parents! Parents are to teach the Word of God to their children. Verse seven continues, "Talk about them when you sit at home and when you walk along the road, when you lie down and when you get up."

There are opportunities every day to impress the Word in your children. Talk about the Word when you get up, when you drive from place to place, when you relax at home, and before you go to bed.

These verses are talking about a lifestyle. It's not just something you follow on Sunday and Wednesday. It's not just something you follow when it is convenient. It's something that you do every day, all day. For some of you, that means you are going to have to make some time for your children by turning the television or the radio or your phone off. Not only that, you need to sit down and talk to your children face-to-face. What a radical concept, I know.

The truth is you cannot impart things into your children that you are not willing to do yourself. You are the best examples that your children will have. When my girls were born, I quickly realized that if I wanted them to grow and marry a man of God, first I needed to be a man of God. If I didn't want them to date jerks, I needed to treat their mother the way I wanted some young man to treat them one day.

I believe with all my heart what is good for the goose is good for the gander. The same set of rules that applies to you, applies to your children as well. We all must model the behavior we want our kids to follow.

CHAPTER 3

HOW TO FAIL
FORWARD

When you as a parent make a mistake or fail, the way you handle it is the way your kids will learn to handle it. As Christians, when we make a mistake, we go to the Word, correct the error and vow to never make that same mistake again. This is the key to failing forward. This is the example that trains your kids to handle their own mistakes. As you fail forward, you will see your children do the same.

Additionally, you must make a choice to not let circumstances slow you down. Choose to think God's thoughts by lining your thoughts up with the Word of God. Choose to do the right thing according to what the Word instructs you. It's all about choices.

In order to properly train our kids to fail forward, we must first learn how to fail forward in our own lives. The first step after you make a mistake is to immediately admit you were wrong. Don't put it off. Tell your kids, "I blew it."

Let me tell you something else. Don't write your children a letter. Don't put it in a memo. It is vital that you do it face-to-face, and do it now.

I learned early in life that it is better to quickly admit a mistake instead of putting it off. As a child I knew that I would not get in nearly as much trouble if I went ahead and told the truth right away. When I would lie to get out of something, not only did I eventually get punished for what I did, I also got punished for lying. I don't know about you, but for me two spankings are bad. Double your pleasure, double your fun, but don't double your spankings.

Two wrongs never make a right. As parents we must teach our children to tell the truth the first time. But remember, if kids don't see this modeled in their parents' lives, they are not going to do it either.

Now, once you have admitted the mistake, repent. Children need to see that the home is a model of repentance. You see, there's a difference between "I'm sorry I got caught" and true repentance. The word *repent* means to do a one-eighty. It means the person must go in the opposite direction than where they were headed. True repentance says,

"I'm sorry. I realize this behavior is wrong, and now I am going to do the opposite of what I was doing."

Repentance is what salvation is all about. When I became a Christ follower, I was taken out of the kingdom of darkness and put into the Kingdom of Light. I changed directions. My actions were totally different.

When I got saved, I didn't really know the Word. I was just smart enough to realize that anything I had been doing up until when I asked Jesus into my heart, had to stop. I didn't hear a sermon about not using drugs or making lifestyle changes. I just knew I needed the Savior, and I needed to do the opposite of what I used to do. Right now, your challenge is to model this same choice for your kids seven days a week, not just when you're around other Christians.

One of the key ingredients in repentance is taking responsibility for your actions. We have all had the baseball-through-the-window experience. At the moment it happens, you have a choice to admit you were the one swinging the bat. Truly taking responsibility means that if you broke it, you must pay for it.

Growing up, I did some really stupid stuff. But one of the things that caused me to quit making mistakes was the fact that I could not afford them. I knew that when I made a mistake, I had to say I was sorry, but I also had to earn the money to make restitution.

It is important to realize that our kids are not going to learn this if we do not do whatever it takes in our own lives. Children must see you offer to repay, even work extra, to pay the person back when you make a mistake.

Some will say, "Well, I'm under grace. I've been forgiven." Yes, but sin has its consequences. I know people that are gloriously saved...in prison. They have repented for their actions, but they must still serve time because of what they did.

Our kids need to understand that Mom and Dad are going to forgive them, but there is still a consequence to pay. Where are children going to learn this? The answer is easy: at home. When you make a mistake, whether it is on the job or at home, admit it and offer to pay for it.

I had an intern years ago that decided he was going to make overhead transparencies. The only problem was that he did not grab overhead transparencies; he just grabbed some plastic sheets that he thought were transparencies. Then he put them in the copier and began to make copies. When the first two or three didn't work, he did what any young person would do, he just kept putting more in. Before long, the entire copier was all messed up.

I was so proud of this kid because he offered to pay for his mistake. He understood that he should have asked how to make overhead transparencies. But when he broke the copier, he took responsibility and offered to do whatever it took to pay for his mistake. We didn't make him pay for it, but we were glad that he offered. That was not something he learned on his own. His parents put that in him. That is something that I want in my children, too, but I believe the only way it will happen is if they see a living example first.

CHAPTER 4

MAKE A PLAN

Just because you admit you've done something wrong, it doesn't mean everything is okay right away. When you as a parent have taken responsibility in front of your children for a mistake, and after you have repented to God, then the next step is to come up with a plan to rectify or correct the mistake.

One of the greatest ways to form a plan is to begin with the end in mind. When I began constructing a plan for how I wanted to raise my kids, I had to look at where I wanted them to be when they grew up and work backward. So I made a list of everything I wanted them to be as an adult. I wanted them to be saved, so I wrote that down. I wanted them to be filled with the Holy Spirit, so I wrote that down. I wanted them to be prayer warriors, to be able to share their faith and lead someone to the Lord, to be givers and to develop a love and respect for God's Word. So I wrote all of those things down.

I wrote down a similar list for the kids in my children's church. And when I brought in wonderful children's workers, I only used adults whose lives were living examples of those choices. Once I had role models, those teachers could share God's Word in the classrooms, and the kids would not only be hearing the Word, but they would be seeing it as well. When those kids both heard the Word and saw the teachers modeling Christian qualities, their lives began to change.

The exact same thing works in parenting. When we will teach kids God's Word and model that behavior with our own lives, then our kids will become godly and begin to walk those things out. What's important is that we are willing to model it first.

Once you have made a plan to correct your mistake, it is important that you walk it out. If correction or discipline is needed, take it and prove yourself faithful. There have been so many times in my life that I have been forgiven, but at the same time I had to prove that I could be trusted again. After you are forgiven is the crucial time to prove that you have truly repented.

Allow people to watch you begin to walk in the opposite direction. Walking it out takes time, and I know it is hard to be patient. But realize that God is a God of second chances:

> He mocks proud mockers but gives grace to the humble.
>
> *Proverbs 3:34 niv*

The lowly are the humble. If you will humble yourself, walk out your plan and stick with it, God will exalt you. James 4:6 niv says that He will give us more grace:

> God opposes the proud but gives grace to the humble.

First Peter 5:5 niv says, "Young men, in the same way be submissive to those who are older. All of you, clothe yourselves with humility toward one another, because,

'God opposes the proud but gives grace to the humble.'"

You must walk it out. Realize that you have to prove yourself, and remember that God is the Restorer. If you will do what is right, He will restore you.

Sometimes we may think the steps we take to correct the problem are not justified or necessary, but I know that God always honors His Word. Go ahead and prove yourself faithful. God is going to settle the score. He will fix it. It might take a year, might take two years; it might take three years, but the information will get back to where it needs to be. God will fix it, but we need to humble ourselves and do what is right, no matter what.

CHAPTER

5

KEEP OTHERS OUT

In the seventies, comedian Flip Wilson coined the phrase, "The devil made me do it." While the devil may tempt us a certain way, we are the ones who make the choice to put action to the temptation. Likewise, when you make a mistake, don't blame others for it, and don't make excuses. Just take ownership of it. You set the example that when it is your fault, it's your fault. The end. This teaches your children the proper way to handle their mistakes.

Similarly, once you make a mistake, don't talk about the mistake or the incident, especially if it involves others. People who talk about their problems are trying to draw sympathy or loyalty. This happens frequently at work when people try to get coworkers to take sides. And it also happens a lot within the family.

At home watch your child's attitude after the discipline has been given. Do not tolerate the poor-old-me syndrome and the mean-Mom-and-Dad attitude. Children will always try to draw sympathy, but the Bible calls it "sowing seeds of discord." Proverbs 6:16-19 nkjv clearly tells us that sowing seeds of discord is an abomination to God:

> These six things the Lord hates,
> Yes, seven are an abomination to Him:

A proud look,
A lying tongue,
Hands that shed innocent blood,
A heart that devises wicked plans,
Feet that are swift in running to evil,
A false witness who speaks lies,
And one who sows discord among brethren.

Another point to remember after making a mistake is to not let the mistake affect how you relate to those around you. That means, when you make a mistake, don't run away from people. Also, don't let that mistake cause you to dodge or withdraw from others. Acknowledge the wrong and move on. Don't let it put a wedge in your relationships.

Listen to me. No one likes a pouter. They don't like one who is four, and they don't like one who is forty-four. Don't pout. You can grow up no matter how old you are. You are the only one who can take control of your actions and let them reflect a mature choice.

Additionally, train your children to take their thumbs out of their mouths by not letting your mistakes affect how you relate to others. Put your big-boy or big-girl pants on and treat others maturely. If you get corrected, you face that person *the next day*. Don't run away from them. When you are corrected, it's a sign that you are loved and cared for.

In your family, work hard to let your children know that just because they make a mistake, your relationship with them is not affected. You still love them and care for them with all of your heart. Unconditional love is the trait you want to model; it's a trait that your heavenly Father demonstrates to you, so it's important that you reflect God's love to your family as well.

ENCOURAGE YOURSELF IN THE LORD

One of my favorite stories in the Bible is found in 1 Samuel 30:6 niv, "David was greatly distressed because the men were talking of stoning him; each one was bitter in spirit because of his sons and daughters." This passage is talking about when David and his men came back from war only to find the enemy had invaded their camp and stolen all of their stuff including their wives and children.

Now I understand that these men were upset, but let's think about it for just a minute. David had more reason to be upset than anyone else. Since he was king, he had more stuff than anyone. He not only had more stuff, but he also had more wives and more children. Although everyone suffered big losses, David suffered the greatest. But rather than sitting back and feeling sorry for himself, verse six continues, "But David encouraged himself in the Lord his God." I love that verse.

I want you to realize something: When you make a mistake and repent, you need to encourage yourself in the Lord too. Don't get down on yourself; encourage yourself. If you will model this behavior for your kids, it will teach them that when they mess up, they serve a God of a second chance. They will also learn that Mom and Dad believe in them and are going to give them a second chance. But before they learn this, remember, you must first believe in yourself and encourage yourself in the things of the Lord.

In the midst of this process, never quit or give up. When I think about a guy who had reason to give up, I think about Joseph in the Bible. Consider everything that happened in his life. He certainly had a reason to say, "Man, this doesn't work." He shared his dreams with his family and the next thing he knew, he was in slavery. But it wasn't long, and he was out of slavery and in charge of a household. Then something happened again. He got on top, but in the next moment, he was in prison. Joseph hung in there, and soon he found himself running the prison. God was able to use Joseph for his God-given purpose because despite all the hardships, Joseph never quit.

The best thing we can instill in our children is to never quit or give up. When things are hard, when situations are not going the way they need to, we should never quit. And when our kids see us pressing forward, they will also keep going after they make mistakes.

To me, a dumb person is not a person that makes mistakes; it's a person that makes the same mistake again and again. You have heard the old saying, "Fool me once, shame on you. Fool me twice, shame on me." But really, when I make the same mistake again and again, it is just shame on me every time. Why? Because I need to correct it and learn from it. This is the behavior we must train our children to follow.

Ten Steps to Handling a Mistake God's Way

1. When you make a mistake, admit it face-to-face.
2. Repent.
3. Come up with a plan to correct the mistake.
4. Walk the plan out.
5. Don't blame others when you make a mistake.
6. Don't talk about the mistake to draw sympathy or loyalty from others.
7. Don't let your mistake affect how you relate to those around you.
8. Encourage yourself in the Lord.
9. Don't give up.
10. Don't make the same mistake twice.

CHAPTER 7

TRAINING YOUR CHILDREN

There's a word that businesses understand better than we in the church. That word is *training*. When you begin a job where training is offered, you are put next to someone who knows how to do the job well. That person actually has hands-on experience, so they know what works and what does not.

When training begins, you are to watch and learn from that person. You ask questions and allow them to demonstrate that job to you. Then, little by little, they turn things over to you. The whole time they are turning it over to you, they are watching to make sure you do it right. As a trainee, you know that it is their way or the highway. Your trainer makes corrections along the way and teaches you so that in the end you know exactly how to complete that job.

Unfortunately, in the church it doesn't always happen this way. For example, let's say someone is willing to teach a children's church class. The ministry leader gives them a Sunday school book, throws them in a classroom, and tells them to not come out until Jesus comes back. Three years later, that volunteer has recruited a helper. The new recruit comes to the class, walks in, and the teacher in the class runs out hollering,

"I quit!"

Immediately, the person recruited to be a helper turns into a leader. That's not training; it's dumping.

Just like children's church workers need training, children need to be trained by their parents as well.

When our girls, Yancy and Whitney, were born, Julie and I made the decision that she would be a stay-at-home mom. This was a decision Julie's parents had made, and it was a desire of her heart. We never regretted this decision.

Also, it was a desire of my heart to give Julie a day off from the kids, just like I had a day off every week from my job. So every Saturday, the girls hung out with me. Saturdays were my day to prepare the church for service, so I'd take the girls to the church to help me set up. While we were working, I learned that I had to do more than just give orders to my girls in order for them to do it correctly. I not only had to show them how to do it, but I also had to explain why they had to do it a certain way, and I had to observe them while they worked and make sure they did it the right way. You see training is more show than tell.

Proverbs 22:6, a familiar verse to parents and children says, "Train up a child in the way he should go: and when he is old, he will not depart from it." We have a responsibility to do more than just give our children lip service; we must train them. The process of training our children begins with us as parents. We are the models. After we model the correct behavior for our children, only a few more things are needed to properly train them to discover their God-given potential.

CONSIDER IT JOY

While you train your kids to do the right things, do not let them know that times are hard. The best thing we can do is to follow what God's Word says in James 1:2 niv, "Consider it pure joy, my brothers, whenever you face trials of many kinds." In trials of any kind, we are to consider it joy. That's weird, isn't it? Think about it. When you are facing a trial, consider it pure joy. I know it's not pure joy if you are thinking the way the world thinks, but when you make your thinking line up with God's Word, then you will be able to count it all joy.

Similarly, we know that the testing of our faith develops perseverance. James 1:4 tells us, "But let patience have her perfect work, that ye may be perfect and entire, wanting nothing." That's pretty good, isn't it?

One of the saddest stories I was ever told was about a little boy who took his own life. His parents had gotten into the habit of arguing in front of their son. They argued about everything, but more than any other subject, they argued about their lack of money. This habit not only affected their relationship, but it also affected their son.

This young man was so saddened by his parents' actions that he began to think that his parents might not fuss and fight so much about money if he was not around. He did the unthinkable, and his parents learned an important lesson the hard way. While this might seem harsh, for me it was a constant reminder how my choices, including my conversations with my wife, could have affected my children. No matter how innocent I might have thought a comment or complaint was, I didn't go there in front of my kids.

During the beginning stages of my ministry, Julie and I never talked in front of our children about the financial struggles and challenges we were facing. When we couldn't afford something at that moment, we did not go into a chorus of the song "Poor, Poor, Pitiful Me!" I also never discussed work-related challenges with my girls. If there was something Julie and I needed to discuss, we would wait until the children went to bed. Of course, we wanted our children to use their faith and believe God for things they needed, but we tried to protect them from adult-level stress.

The attitude you model when you go through trials rubs off on your children. Now that my kids are grown, I can share with them some of the trials and challenges we faced when they were younger. Most of the time they tell me that they had no idea those things were going on. And today when they face trials, they follow God's Word and determine to consider it pure joy because they know God will always provide and make things right.

CHAPTER 9

WHERE DO I START?

Training your kids to fail forward is something that all imperfect parents can do. Remember, kids will need some coaching and help along the way. They will not automatically fail forward. So when they make a mistake, there are some easy steps to follow to make their recovery process a positive learning experience.

To begin, when your child makes a mistake, you must confront them in love. But you may argue, "I'm not a confronter." Well, Jesus is our example. He confronted things, so we must also confront our children when they do wrong. And while I have never called my children a "generation of vipers" or a "faithless and perverse generation," I do confront my children in love.

Not one time in all the years I've been in church have I ever turned over a table and run somebody out of the church (I may have thought about it a couple of times, but that's a whole different book). The point is we must not ignore a situation and hope it goes away. Confront it! Let your children know when they have messed up by confronting them.

When you confront them, correct them in love. Correction involves explaining why they are in trouble and what they did wrong.

When I was working in a church in Jackson, Mississippi, I dealt with a father whose boy disobeyed at home but didn't act out in children's church. The father was amazed and didn't understand why the boy acted so differently. Later we learned that at home the consequences for making bad choices were always different. Sometimes the boy would be laughed at and told his behavior was funny, but other times he would get in trouble. On the flip side, at church this boy always made good choices because when he tested the rules, the consequences were always the same.

He was a good kid, but he was confused. You can keep confusion out of your home by confronting and correcting your children with consistency. In order to properly train your children, you must be willing to confront and correct them on a constant basis, not just when you feel like it. Set the guidelines and stick to them.

When you correct your children, never correct them in anger. If necessary, give yourself some time to cool down before you correct them. Be sure that when you are correcting them, you give them the Word and let them know why their actions disagree with the Word. Talk to them about their mistakes without lecturing. Let them know how you have made similar mistakes in your own life.

This means you don't just tell your kids about the time you knocked it out of the park and were very successful. You also need to tell them about how you reacted when you struck out and messed up in life. Let them know you put your pants on one leg at a time just like they do. That way they realize you understand how they are feeling.

Once you have confronted your children, allow them to ask for forgiveness and repent. The greatest thing you can teach your kids is to confess with their mouths when they mess up. The Word says in 1 John 1:9, "If we confess our sins, he is faithful and just to forgive us our sins, and to cleanse us from all unrighteousness." If they don't repent, you need to forgive them but handle the failure more severely. Most importantly, remember kids learn best when they see their role model, you, living it out first.

In the Bible, David is our example of repentance. He was a man after God's own heart. And even though we know that he blew it a lot, he always sought repentance. Our children need to follow that same pattern in their lives.

CHOOSING THE
PROPER PUNISHMENT

My two girls are completely different. Every strong-willed child book that is out describes Yancy. When she was little, she would look at her mom and say, "Spank me some more, Mom." Instead of letting that upset us, we chose to believe that God was going to use that strong will for something good.

Whitney, on the other hand, was totally different. All you had to do was say Whitney's name, and she would spout out,

"Oh I'm sorry. God, forgive me! I'll never do it again!" Then she would break down and start crying, "I don't want to go to Hell!"

We tried to explain to her, "Honey, you are not going to go to Hell. We just need you to clean up your room."

Two totally different responses from two totally different kids made it tempting to base their punishments on the way they each reacted, but we knew it was important to let the punishment fit the crime.

This is a tough one for parents. Sometimes you may be tempted to give your kids the gas chamber or the electric chair, but you must choose a punishment that's appropriate.

Other parents don't believe in punishment at all, but I would encourage you take a look at what the Bible says:

> Folly is bound up in the heart of a child,
> but the rod of discipline will drive it far from him.
>
> *Proverbs 22:15 niv*

> Do not withhold discipline from a child;
> if you punish him with the rod, he will not die.
>
> *Proverbs 23:13 niv*

> The rod of correction imparts wisdom,
> but a child left to himself disgraces his mother.
>
> *Proverbs 29:15 niv*

The Bible doesn't say you're going to kill your children by punishing them; it says your children will be harmed if you don't punish them.

On the flip side, some of us parents need to take a chill pill. We need to go back and remember some of the bonehead stuff we did and ask ourselves why our child is acting out. Most of the time it is because the child is acting just like the parents.

After you discipline your child, one of the best things you can do is pray with them. Let them know, "I forgive you, and the Lord forgives you"; and tell them, "You have done what you needed to do by taking your punishment. Now, let's pray." When you are finished praying, give them a hug. Physically show your children that you love them even when they mess up.

OUR FATHER

I purposed that when I had kids, I would be a model of the heavenly Father to my children so they could understand the true nature of God the Father. As a young man I had trouble relating to God because my real dad died when I was three. When I was in college, my mom remarried a wonderful godly man but by that time I was not really living at home anymore. Like me, many people have a hard time relating to their Father God because their earthly fathers were not godly men.

Since I didn't have a father model growing up, the majority of what I learned about fatherhood came from just reading about Father God in Scripture. I learned that my Father God loves me unconditionally, so even when my children disappoint me, I am to show them love. My Father God is a rewarder, so I, too, must look for every possible opportunity to bless my children. My Father God provides for my needs since I am one of His own, so my children always know that they can come to me when they are in need. My Father God rewards obedience, so I make sure to catch my children doing things that are right. My Father God is a protector, so I watch carefully over my girls. My Father God is quick to forgive, and someone His children can call on anytime.

Searching God's Word, I found forty-two verses that specifically talk about what God the Father does for His children. These attributes should serve as a checklist for all parents as they model God to their children:

> God spends time with His children.
> God is our Witness.
> God does not lie.
> God gives.
> God is merciful.
> God tests our love.
> God is with us when we face our enemies.
> God is our Refuge.
> God is our Rock.
> God is gracious and compassionate.
> God is mighty.
> God is strong.
> God is a righteous Judge.
> God is our Help.
> God is our Sustainer.
> God is for us.
> God is good.
> God is holy.
> God is full of compassion.
> God is near.
> God is wise.
> God is faithful.
> God is just.
> God is Love.

Use these as a guide to parent your children. Hug your kids and love on them. Parents, we are the best chance our kids have to know what their Father God is like. You are a living example. Now, go act like it.

CHAPTER 12

FORGIVE AND FORGET

One time, a parent called me up and asked if I would meet with her son to reinforce some things that she and her husband were telling him. She knew that when I taught the kids at church, my team and I were teaching the same principles that they the parents were teaching at home. She also understood that when children hear from somebody other than Mom or Dad, all of the sudden they realize that maybe their parents are not as far off as they thought.

So when this young man heard he was going to tell Brother Jim what he did, he told his mom, "I don't want to go tell Brother Jim what I'm doing. Brother Jim thinks I am wonderful, and I don't want him to know how I really am."

To which his mother replied, "Too bad, I've already told Brother Jim how you really are."

This mom understood the principle that after a child makes a mistake and repents, neither the parents nor the children's pastor is to treat that child any differently. It empowered this young man to repent because he learned that true forgiveness would follow.

Another method to aid in successfully training your children is to always point out to them what they have done right. Speak good things about your children. It begins with how you view them. Start looking at your child not as half empty, but as half full. Yes, there are things that need fixing, but focus on the good by talking about it. Train yourself to look at them positively, and speak out when you see the good, even when it is a normal everyday thing.

A few years ago, I was vacationing in California with my wife and two girls. When I went into a popular retail store, I noticed the people that worked there were the kind of folks that got a job based on how many tattoos and piercings they had. They looked like a canvas with drawings all over their bodies. When I walked out of the store, I handed each one of my girls a hundred-dollar bill. They looked at me kind of funny, so I said, "Thank you for not putting your Mom and me through what the employees in this store put their parents through."

I don't know about you, but when you are looking at somebody that is 16 to 18 years old and has 27 tattoos and 400 earrings, and that is just in their nose, it makes me want to give my children a love offering.

Catch your children doing something right and brag on them. Let's start telling our kids what they are doing right. Let's reward them for good behavior. My model of this is my Father God. He is a rewarder of those that diligently seek Him. He will correct us, but He will also reward us when we do things right. We need to be the same way with our kids.

Finally, when our kids make a mistake, don't bring up that mistake again. Let go, and don't talk about it. If they truly ask for repentance and for the Lord to forgive them, the Lord is not going to bring it up again, so why should we as parents? They still must walk out their repentance and earn our respect again, but we don't need to talk about their failure. We focus on the good and talk about it all the time.

Ten Steps to Dealing With Your Children's Mistakes

1. Confront them face-to-face.
2. Correct and explain what they did wrong.
3. Allow your kids to ask forgiveness and repent.

4. Forgive them and give them a chance to make it right.
5. Let the punishment fit the crime.
6. Pray with them, and give them a hug.
7. Don't be overly critical while they work out their plan.
8. Don't treat them differently after they mess up.
9. Look for ways to make them feel good about themselves.
10. Don't bring up the mistake again.

CONCLUSION

You may be asking, "Where do I start?" Well, it all starts with you. As a dad, an educator, and a leader, when the Lord shows me something I need to do differently, it's my job to be man enough to start that change. For you, the change starts now.

The first step toward change is to go back over the 10 steps I've given you to follow when dealing with your children's mistakes. Use the list like a test. Which of these 10 steps do you need to work on? It's never too late to make right choices or to make corrections to your parenting skills. It's always the right time to do the right thing.

When you blow it with your kids, admit it. Ask their forgiveness. John 13:15 niv says, "I have set you an example that you should do as I have done for you." Who said that? Jesus did! Jesus didn't say, "I'm going to live one way and you live another." No, He modeled it and said that He's shown us what to do; now we have to make the choice to do it.

It's up to you to do the same thing with your children. First Timothy 4:12 niv is a scripture that people love to quote, especially when they are young:

> Don't let anyone look down on you because you are young,
> but set an example for the believers in speech, in life, in
> love, in faith and in purity.

If you want your children to know how to live God's Word, be the example. Be willing to let your kids know that you're going to model right behavior even when you blow it. Show them that there is not a different set of rules for you than there is for them. If you do these things, I believe with all my heart that God will help you be a better parent. Your kids are going to learn how to fail forward when you set the example.

PRAYER
OF SALVATION

God loves you- no matter who you are or what your past is. He loves you so much that He gave His one and only begotten Son for you. The Bible tells us"...whoever believes in him shall not perish but have eternal life" (John 3:16). Jesus laid down His life and rose again so that we could spend eternity with Him in heaven and experience His absolute best on earth. If you would like to receive Jesus into your life, say the following prayer out loud and mean it from your heart.

Heavenly Father, I come to You admitting that I am a sinner. Right now, I choose to turn away from sin, and I ask You to cleanse me of all unrighteousness. I believe that Your Son, Jesus, died on the cross to take away my sins. I also believe that He rose again from the dead so that I might be forgiven of my sins and be made righteous through faith in Him. I call upon the name of Jesus Christ to be the Savior and Lord of my life. Jesus, I choose to follow You and ask that you fill me with the power of the Holy Spirit. I declare that I am a child of God. I am free from sin and full of the righteousness of God. I am saved in Jesus' name. Amen

If you prayed this prayer to receive Jesus Christ as your Savior, please contact us at our website at www.jimwideman.com and let us know about your decision.

Or you may write to us at
Jim Wideman Ministries, Inc.
2441 Q Old Fort Parkway #354
Murfreesboro, TN 37128

Meet Jim Wideman

Jim Wideman is an internationally recognized voice in children's and family ministry. He is a much-sought-after speaker, teacher, author, personal leadership coach, and ministry consultant who has over 30 years experience in helping churches thrive.

Having served in five dynamic churches Jim understands what it takes to grow exciting, relevant ministries to people of all ages. For 17 years Jim led one of America's largest local church children's ministry in Tulsa, OK. Jim has also held various other positions in addition to children ministry throughout his career giving him a background in almost every area of the local church and Christian school. Jim currently serves as Associate Pastor at World Outreach Church in Murfreesboro, TN where he oversees the next generation and family ministries.

In addition to working in a local church Jim has successfully trained hundreds of thousands of Children's ministry leaders from all denominations and sizes of congregations in conferences and seminars around the world. Jim is considered an innovator, pioneer and father in the modern children's ministry movement. He also currently serves as president of "The American Children's Ministry Association," as well as president of Jim Wideman Ministries and is one of the executive editors of K! Magazine. The International Network of Children's Pastors awarded Jim the "Excellence in Ministry Award" in 1989 for his outstanding work in Children's Ministry, and Children's Ministry Magazine in 2001 honored him as one of ten "Pioneers of the Decade" in children's ministry.

Jim created the Children's Ministers Leadership Club in 1995 that is known today as "the Club" which has touched thousands of ministry leaders each month. This monthly audio leadership resource is still impacting leaders and causing them to think differently and become better leaders now! In 2007 Jim introduced a personal mentorship program called Infuse where he and a hand-picked-group-of-leaders coach and mentor 20 leaders for a year. (A new group of 20 start every six months)

Jim has one burning desire and that is to help others become better leaders. Jim believes his matching orders are to spend the rest of his life taking what he has learned about leadership and ministry and pour it into the next generation of children's, youth, and family ministry leaders.

For more information go to www.jimwideman.com

What others are saying about Jim...

"I have watched Jim Wideman for a number of years. You can trust his heart and his counsel as a leader who has a passion to see churches succeed in reaching the next generation. His experience at helping churches navigate through change and develop problem solving techniques makes him a valuable asset to any church or ministry. Jim has the mind of an administrator, the heart of a pastor, the wit of a comedian, and the soul of a musician. I always know when I'm on my way spend time with Jim, I am going to walk away warmed, motivated, entertained and equipped to be a better leader and thinker."

– **Reggie Joiner**, *Re-Think Group*

"Jim is a walking encyclopedia of information concerning ministry and management in the local church. Best known for his unique ability to recruit, train, and retain both employees and volunteers, Jim is a highly creative individual who meets challenges head-on. As one of America's top leaders in the area of children's ministry, his knowledge of daily operations in the local church is unmatched. I strongly recommend Jim Wideman as both a consultant and seminar instructor."

– **Joe McGee**, *Joe McGee Ministries // Tulsa, OK*

"I always watch for the leader who can lead us through the challenges of our complicated world and Jim Wideman is one of those unique men. He can lead without compromising the integrity of the mission. Excellence and value are obvious expressions when describing the leadership of Jim Wideman. Personally, I have known him for over 20 years and have admired his creativity as a gifted thinker and communicator. Some people talk about doing it. Jim

has done it. I highly recommend Jim Wideman for whatever creative venue you are wanting to advance to the next
level."

– **Steve Dixon**, *Senior Pastor,*
Christian Life Cathedral // Fayetteville, AR

Other books from jimwideman.com

Children's Ministry In The 21st Century
Volunteers That Stick
Children's Ministry Leadership-the you-can-do-it-guide
Children's Ministry That Works
Connect With Your Kids

CPSIA information can be obtained at www.ICGtesting.com

224641LV00001B/3/P

9 780881 445060